LEGAL INSIDER'S GUIDE TO SAN DIEGO DIVORCE, LEGAL SEPARATION & PATERNITY

LEGAL STRATEGIES AND TECHNIQUES
TO PROTECT YOUR LEGAL RIGHTS
AND TO TRY AND OBTAIN
YOUR LEGAL GOALS

WRITTEN BY AN EXPERIENCED
SAN DIEGO FAMILY LAW ATTORNEY

ROY M. DOPPELT, ESQUIRE

Legal Insider's Guide to San Diego Divorce,
Legal Separation and Paternity

Published in the United States

Manufactured in the United States of America

ISBN: 978-0-615-32331-2

DEDICATION

This book is dedicated to the San Diego County Family Law Judiciary without whose efforts the resolution of citizen's most difficult issues would not be possible. The author is honored to have appeared before these Judges and wants to thank them for their hard work and dedication to public service. The Judges work hard to administer justice in a fair and impartial manner and are often criticized when they should be praised.

TABLE OF CONTENTS

INTRODUCTION

If you are currently involved in a divorce, whether contested or uncontested, a legal separation or a paternity case, the information in this book will be invaluable to you. I will give you "inside information" into the family law court in San Diego, California and will also give you techniques and strategies based on my education, training and experience which will assist you in protecting your rights and trying to obtain your goals. It is imperative that you list your goals before starting this process since the strategies and techniques will be dependent on your goals. All cases are "unique". However, the law which applies to each case is the same for all persons. The above questions are samples of some the author has heard over many years and compiled these into an easy-to-use reference guide for educational purposes only. My hope is that many find this useful and that it assists them during a very stressful and difficult time in their lives.

Some sections of this book have been lifted "in toto" from other articles and publications of the author and some are unique to this book. This book is a compilation of information in an easy-to-use book which you can take with you and read at your convenience.

CHAPTER ONE
SHOULD I HIRE AN ATTORNEY?

The first issue is whether you will represent yourself or hire an attorney. There are advantages and disadvantages to both. The advantages of hiring an attorney is that you will have an experienced professional counseling and assisting you. In addition, the attorney will prepare all of the pleadings and make sure they are filed in a timely manner and served in accordance with the local rules on current judicial council pleading forms. This is a very difficult area of the law in which to be a client, and there is a "peace of mind" in knowing that you are being represented by an aggressive attorney who will give you honest and frank advice and always look out for your best interests. Another advantage is that a divorce, legal separation, or paternity is a very emotional case, and it is not a recommended strategy to make decisions based on emotions. An attorney can help you be objective, which will help your case. The disadvantage is that hiring an attorney will cost money. The advantage of representing yourself is that there are no legal fees and you can use the money you would pay to an attorney for your own expenses and family. The disadvantage is that you are emotionally involved, do not know the law, and do not know what is a realistic expectation. Many attorneys will offer a free and confidential consultation in which your specific case can be discussed so that you will have a realistic expectation. No attorney can guarantee the result of any case. However, some realistic expectations should be able to be discussed. For example, in San Diego all parents must attend the mandatory mediation before a Judge makes an order for a parenting plan [custody and visitation orders] with the exception of emergency orders due to abuse, neglect or molestation. An attorney can discuss with you the procedure for this and in this book specific strategies are discussed for the mandatory mediation. Ultimately, of course, it is your decision whether or not to hire an attorney.

CHAPTER TWO
HOW DO I AVOID MAKING A MISTAKE WHEN CHOOSING AN ATTORNEY?

The best way, in my opinion, is to obtain a referral from a friend, relative, or co worker who was a client of the attorney and can tell you first hand their experience. Another way is to obtain a referral from a bar certified referral service by the State Bar of California. This ensures that the attorney has a valid license to practice law in California, has malpractice insurance, and has experience in family law. The four bar certified referral services which are listed in this book also offer all callers a one half-hour free consultation with a qualified attorney. As with all information in this book, phone numbers change so I have also placed their website addresses for your convenience. For disclosure purposes, the author is, or has been, on all four of these panels:

San Diego County Bar Association **619-231-8585**
www.sdbca.org

San Diego North County Bar Association **760-758-4755**
www.lawyerreferral.org

Attorney Search Network **800-215-1190**
www.getareferral.com

Attorney Referral Service **877-277-2778**
www.lawyerreferral.com

In addition, there are other ways to find out about attorneys and their qualifications. A very respected company is called Martindale-Hubbell and their website is *www.lawyers.com.* They rate attorneys through a process called Peer Review Rating and also rate attorneys and law firms with a rating of AV, BV or CV. This is an independent and unbiased source of information. Of course, before hiring an attorney, it is crucial to meet with the attorney who will be handling your case personally to make sure that your personalities are compatible. Look at the appearance of the office and whether it is professional. Look at the appearance of the attorney and her/his professionalism. Does the attorney have a paralegal? Does the attorney have research programs to keep current on the law? Does the attorney attend family law seminars annually to keep her/his knowledge updated? Family law practice is difficult for both clients and attorneys so all of these are very important. There are many other ways to choose an attorney [specialist; geographical location; local reputation; etc.] and all are appropriate. You do not want to have "buyer's remorse" when it comes to such an important decision.

CHAPTER THREE
SHOULD I HIRE A MEDIATOR INSTEAD OF HIRING AN ATTORNEY?

In San Diego, there are many options for legal representation for divorce. There are five courts in San Diego which handle divorce cases. There are two in San Diego, one in North County, one in El Cajon, and one in the South Bay. The first option is to hire an attorney to protect your rights and to try and obtain your legal goals. This is an attorney who will represent only you. The second option is to hire a mediator. However, this attorney [mediator] will not only represent you but will represent your spouse. As with all strategies and techniques, there are advantages and disadvantages with each approach and these are explained in more detail below. This is not to be confused with child custody and child visitation mandatory mediation under the Family Law Code and in practice in all the courts in San Diego.

Divorce Attorney Advantages: You have an attorney representing your interests. In our firm, we represent only one spouse and never both in a divorce matter. There is an actual conflict of interest in representing both clients in a divorce case.

Divorce Attorney Disadvantages: You will each have to pay for one attorney which can increase legal fees and costs. You will also have two attorneys involved, rather than one attorney, which can lead to increased tensions and conflict if the two attorneys cannot work well together.

Mediator Advantages: You will have to pay for only one attorney. This may lead to reduced tensions and conflicts if two attorneys cannot work together.

Mediator Disadvantages: You do not have an attorney representing only your interests. Since your interests are adverse, the mediator's suggestions for support payments [for example] may not be what is in your best interests. In addition, if the case does not settle in mediation, then your legal fees will increase since the mediator cannot represent either spouse in a pending divorce due to the confidential information shared in the mediation. As such, if the case does not settle in mediation, you and your spouse will then each have to hire an attorney which will mean three attorney fees instead of two. As an example, in a personal injury legal action, if you are driving on the freeway and a drunk driver hits your car with you driving and your spouse in the passenger seat, then both of your interests are exactly the same. There is no conflict of interest in an attorney representing both of you since your cause of action is only against the driver and/or registered owner of the vehicle which hit you and not against each other. In a divorce legal action, conversely, you are adversarial litigants. In fact, in support cases, the payor has a financial incentive to pay less and the payee has a financial incentive to receive more. As there is an inverse relationship between the percentage of custody and visitation and the amount of support, the adversity can intensify. All strategies and techniques have advantages and disadvantages and these can only be properly implemented upon informed and intelligent decisions.

CHAPTER FOUR
WHAT SHOULD I BRING AND HOW DO I PREPARE FOR MY FIRST MEETING WITH AN ATTORNEY TO MAKE SURE ALL OF THE INFORMATION IS DISCUSSED?

The attorney, at the initial consultation, should discuss strategies and techniques based on her/his experience, education and training to try and protect your legal rights and to try and obtain your legal goals. It is important for you to consider what your top goals are for your case. The attorney can then give a frank and honest opinion as to the realistic expectations based upon your individual facts and circumstances. While the law which applies is the same to all, the facts of each case are unique. One suggestion is to write down your top five goals in preparation for your initial consultation with the attorney. If you have minor children, it is important to consider whether or not you should stay or vacate the residence. Some parties can live together during their divorce or legal separation and some cannot. In either event, the legal standard the Judge uses is the "best interests" of the child[ren] and this includes stability, bonding, frequent and continuing contact; co-operation or non-cooperation in the parenting plan; abuse; molestation; neglect; and many other factors. For many persons, the most important goal in their case concerns custody and visitation and their parenting plan. At your initial consultation, the attorney will calculate the spousal and/or child support for you, using the Disso Master Program. This will give you a realistic expectation of the support so that you can intelligently plan for the future post-separation. If you have assets and/or debts, then the division of these will need to occur. For the initial consultation, it is a good idea to bring the following: a list of each asset and when it was acquired; a list of each debt and when it was acquired; the value of each asset when it was acquired and how; all bills which are part of your total monthly expenses; documents relating to any business interests, copies of all deeds, mortgages, revocable living trusts, estate plans, IRA's, KEOGH's, vested and non-vested stock options, bank accounts, brokerage accounts, pensions, retirements, profit sharing, tax returns, and any other accounts you have access to. In many cases, some or all of these are not available at the initial consultation and this is understandable. In many cases, one spouse does not know what the true assets and valuations are. The attorney, at the initial consultation, can discuss strategies to discover such as review of the Schedule of Assets and Debts of the other spouse, written discovery, request for the production of documents, request for admissions, depositions, asset searches, private investigators, and other more advanced strategies which are discussed later in this book. It is crucial to have your initial consultation before taking any actions since you can only make the best decision with an informed and intelligent analysis.

CHAPTER FIVE
WHAT ISSUES WILL I HAVE TO DEAL WITH IN MY CASE?

Every case is different but the laws remain steady. Thus, it is important to consult with an attorney. As already discussed, some issues may not apply to your case. Likewise, you may encounter| issues that are not mentioned below. If your case is a divorce or legal separation, you will have to address the following: custody, visitation, child support, spousal support, division of assets and debts which include real estate, personal property, jewelry, household furniture, antiques, coin collections, vehicles, boats; trailers, savings accounts, checking accounts, credit union accounts, deposit accounts, cash, tax refunds, safety deposit boxes, life insurance with a cash surrender value [whole life policy], stocks, bonds, secured notes, mutual funds, retirement accounts, pension accounts, profit sharing, vested and non-vested stock options, restricted stock units, annuities, IRA, STRS, PERS, 403B, 401K, military retirement, accounts receivable, unsecured notes, business interests, partnerships, corporations, student loans, taxes owed, any support arrears, unsecured loans, secured loans, real estate loans, vehicle loans, retirement loans, third party loans, credit cards and others.

If your case is a paternity, then the only issues will be custody, visitation, and child support. This makes the case less complicated in many respects. However, custody and visitation [parenting plan] are normally the most contentious issues in any case. There can also be the issue of attorney fees in all three types of cases above.

CHAPTER SIX
WHAT IS THE DIFFERENCE BETWEEN A LEGAL SEPARATION AND DIVORCE?

Many people are confused about the difference between the two and what the advantages and disadvantages of each are. In general, both are exactly the same with one important difference: with a legal separation judgment, you cannot ever remarry unless you file for a divorce and obtain a divorce judgment. In my opinion there are two factual patterns which lend themselves to a legal separation over a divorce. First, if there are religious convictions such that the spouses will not divorce, then this allows them to live separately and apart in a legal manner with a judgment of legal separation, which terminates the community property laws being applied as the marriage continues and as the parties are still legally married. As stated above, there is no difference other than legal status [married versus unmarried] and a legal separation judgment has exactly the same provisions as a divorce judgment: child custody, child visitation, spousal support, child support, division of assets and debts. As such, both spouses can go on with their lives. Both parties after judgment in a legal separation, should immediately execute new estate plans including a revocable living trust if they own a residence or have assets over $100,000 [combined] in most instances. Since the parties are still married legally, this is mandatory to protect the rights of the separated spouses in the event of death. This also needs to be accomplished in a divorce however, in the judgment of divorce, the parties are no longer "spouses" for inheritance issues. Second, if there is a member spouse who has health insurance coverage and a non-member spouse who does not have health insurance coverage and the non-member spouse has significant health issues or is not employable and cannot obtain private insurance due to the cost. This legal separation is normally used when the spouses are 60 years of age and above and have no intentions of remarrying and are separating for other reasons. If there is a legal separation, a divorce can always be filed. However, this will take additional time and costs. So the vast majority of petitions filed in family law court are for divorce and not legal separation.

CHAPTER SEVEN
WHAT DOES PROCEDURAL POSTURE MEAN AND WHY IS IT SO IMPORTANT TO MY CASE?

For family law in San Diego, the procedural posture of your case will determine your rights under the law and what strategies you can implement and which are appropriate. To start a divorce, legal separation or paternity case, you must file the petition and summons in the court house in which you or your spouse are residents. In San Diego, either you or your spouse must be a resident of California for six months and the County of San Diego for three months in order to file for a dissolution in San Diego County. However, there is no such requirement for a legal separation. As there are five family law court houses in San Diego County, you will need to make sure you are filing in the correct court house. This gives the Court power and authority and jurisdiction to make orders in accordance with the law. In a case for divorce and legal separation, this also results in the issuance of automatic temporary restraining orders for non-sale or non-transfer of assets and accounts and also prevents children from being removed from the State of California without an order or written agreement of the parties. In a paternity case, the same restrictions for removal of the children from the State of California apply. In addition, if the case is pre-judgment, then you have more rights than if the case is post-judgment since the right to a trial only applies to pre-judgment. There are no jury trials in family law in San Diego and all trials are heard by a Judge. If the case is post-judgment, normally, a change of circumstances needs to occur for a Judge to modify an existing order and there is no right to a trial. Furthermore, if the case is pre-judgment, your discovery options are much broader than post-judgment and this is discussed in more detail.

If your case is pre-judgment, then the procedural posture will normally follow this example: filing of petition and summons; service of petition and summons; responsive pleadings filed and served; an order to show cause for temporary orders such as custody, visitation, spousal support, child support, temporary exclusive use of the residence and/or vehicles and attorney fees; status conference; case management conference; mandatory settlement conference and trial. Most cases do not go to trial. Over 90% settle without a trial and many cases also settle with no court hearings and without the need for the entire above procedural posture. However, it is very important to understand this since your rights are determined by which procedural posture stage your case is in. In addition, if your case is post judgment, there are strict time periods in which you can ask the Judge to set aside the judgment if you do not feel it was in accordance with the law. This is a very complicated procedure and will not be discussed in detail in this book. However, all of the grounds and time periods are contained in Family Law Code Section 2122.

CHAPTER EIGHT
WHERE ARE THE COURT HOUSES FOR FAMILY LAW AND WHAT ARE THE HOURS AND HOLIDAYS?

As the court schedule changes all the time, please make sure to verify it. Many people take time off work and travel to the court house - only to find they are too early or too late or the court house is closed. The website address for the San Diego Superior Court is **www.sdcourt.ca.gov** and you can verify the below as necessary. As of the writing of this book, the below information is correct. It is important to check dates and hours since the Court may close on some holidays which are observed only by the federal government, others only by the state government, and some which are observed by both. The hours that the facilities are open are as follows: Vista, Chula Vista, El Cajon open at 7:30am. Family Court on 6th and Madge Bradley opens at 8:00am. The hours that the business office is open are different. For the two court houses in San Diego downtown, El Cajon, Vista and Chula Vista, the hours are from 8:30am to 3:30pm. This is when pleadings can be filed. The holidays may fall on different days of the week each year, but they are listed as follows: New Year's Day; Martin Luther King, Jr. Birthday; Lincoln's Birthday; Presidents' Day; Cesar Chavez Day; Memorial Day; Independence Day; Labor Day; Columbus Day; Veterans' Day; Thanksgiving Day; Day after Thanksgiving and Christmas Day. Currently, starting September 16, 2009, the Courts will also be closed every third Wednesday of the month through June 17, 2010 and a decision will be made in January of 2010 whether to continue this closure for fiscal reasons.

CHAPTER NINE
HOW IS THE DECISION MADE AS TO WHERE OUR CHILD[REN] WILL LIVE?

You want to know how the decision will be made as to where your child[ren] will be living and what the exact parenting plan is. In San Diego, California, this is accomplished by a mediation with Family Court Services if the parents cannot reach an agreement. Of course, it is always best to reach an agreement. However, this does not occur in every case. As such, the dispute resolution method is listed below in some detail.

In California, before a Judge will make an order regarding custody and visitation [absent an emergency such as molestation, abuse, or neglect which normally is accompanied by a Child Protective Service recommendation] the parents must attend mandatory mediation. San Diego is a "recommending" County, as opposed to Orange which is a "non-recommending" County. This is crucial since, in San Diego, if the parents do not reach an agreement, then the mediator will prepare a written report and give a copy to each parent and then a copy to the Judge. In my experience, the San Diego County Judges follow the mediator's recommendation 90%+ of the time, since the mediator is a licensed clinical social worker who is hired by the Court to meet with parents and try to get the parents to reach an agreement and, if not, then to make a written recommendation. Of course, this is a very artificial process since the mediator does not know you, the other parent, or your children. As such, it is crucial to try and have the mediator make the recommendation you would like.

It is important to know what to say and what not to say. The first words out of your mouth should be "I want to reach an agreement". This is correct since all parents should want to reach agreements and lessen tensions and conflicts and realize any plan they make is most preferable. In addition, the mediators want parents to reach agreements since they also believe this is the best way to reduce tensions and conflicts. Thus, you will subconsciously allay yourself with the mediator if you first state that you want to reach an agreement. The legal standard which the mediator will look to is the "best interests" test, which is too complicated to entirely discuss in this book. However, the doctrine of stability, bonding, frequent and continuing contact with each parent, cooperation in the parenting plan and other factors are discussed. As such, it is crucial that facts are presented to the mediator as to why you are asking for the parenting plan you want in terms of the best interests of the children and as to the above factors. It is also crucial not to say something which would have the mediator influenced negatively against you without you understanding why. In this book, three issues will be discussed which you should not do in mediation.

The first issue is the inverse relationship between custody and visitation and child support. Again, all insiders know that the more the percentage of visitation the non-custodial parent payor has, the less child support will be paid to the payee. Conversely, the less percentage of visitation the non-custodial parent payor has, the more child support will be paid to the payee. This is a simplification, and there are many other factors to consider. However, in the algebraic formula for the state guideline for child support, which is discussed in greater detail below, the percentage of visitation is a highly weighted factor. My experience is that no parent goes to the mediator and informs the mediator that they do not care about the best interests of their child and that they only want [as the payor] to lower their child support or [as the payee] to raise their child support. Instead, if the parents discuss money and support with the mediator, the mediator may then believe that the reason the parent wants more time [or less time] is due to support issues and not due to the children's best interests. As such, and since the mediators do not make decisions about support in any event, do not discuss money or support with\the mediator.

The second issue is revenge and "getting even" for conduct [either real or perceived] which happened during the marriage relationship, during the divorce, or after the divorce. Again, my experience is that no parent goes to the mediator and informs the mediator that they do not care about the best interests of their child and that they do not care about money, but instead saying they are mad at the other parent and want revenge. If the parent discusses all the negative aspects of the other parent, mediator may believe the reason the parent wants additional time [or less time] is due to revenge. The third issue, and this is one which is very common, is the use of the word "my" when referring to your child or children. If you use the word "my", the mediator may believe that you are an uncaring, possessive and selfish parent and will not cooperate or co-parent. Instead, my suggestion is always to use the word "our" which will demonstrate that you are a caring, promotive, and sharing parent. There are many other issues but only these three will be discussed in this book.

CHAPTER TEN
HOW IS THE AMOUNT OF CHILD SUPPORT DETERMINED AND FOR HOW LONG?

A common question is how much child support will I have to pay or how much child support will I receive? In San Diego, the amount of child support is determined by a computer program called the "Disso Master". This will give a "guideline" child support amount and this is not based on fairness or expenses - only the statutory factors which include [but are not limited to] those listed below. In this way, an attorney in her/his office can assist you in having a realistic expectation without any guarantees, since the attorneys and Judges [in family law courts] use the same program. This program is different if the case is being heard in the Department of Child Support Services by state law. However, the amounts calculated by each program with the same factors are not disparate by a great amount. To show the need to use the program, below is an excerpt of Family Law Code Section 4055 which is used to determine the guideline for child support. For child support calculations, the procedural posture of the case [pre-judgment versus post-judgment] is not a relevant factor as is for spousal support which is explained below.

Fam. Code §4055 provides the following [a full text can be found in the Family Law Code and this is edited for brevity]:

> The statewide uniform guideline for determining child support orders is as follows: CS = K (HN - (H%) (TN).
>
> The components of the formula are as follows:
>
> CS = child support amount.
>
> K = amount of both parents' income to be allocated for child support as set forth in paragraph (3).

HN = high earner's net monthly disposable income.

H% = approximate percentage of time that the high earner has or will have primary physical responsibility for the children compared to the other parent. In cases in which parents have different time-sharing arrangements for different children, H% equals the average of the approxi mate percentages of time the high earner parent spends with each child.

TN = total net monthly disposable income of both parties. (To compute net disposable income, see Section 4059.)

K (amount of both parents' income allocated for child support) equals one plus H% (if H% is less than or equal to 50 percent) or two minus H% (if H% is greater than 50 per cent) times the following fraction:

Total Net Disposable Income Per Month	K
\$0-800	0.20 + TN/16,000
\$801-6,666	0.25
\$6,667-10,000	0.10 + 1,000/TN
Over \$10,000	0.12 + 800/TN

For example, if H% equals 20 percent and the total monthly net disposable income of the parents is \$1,000, K = (1 + 0.20) X 0.25, or 0.30. If H% equals 80 percent and the total monthly net disposable income of the parents is \$1,000, K = (2 - 0.80) X 0.25, or 0.30.

For more than one child, multiply CS by:

2 children	1.6	7 children	2.75
3 children	2	8 children	2.813
4 children	2.3	9 children	2.844
5 children	2.5	10 children	2.86
6 children	2.625		

If the amount calculated under the formula results in a positive number, the higher earner shall pay that amount to the lower earner. If the amount calculated under the formula results in a negative number, the lower earner shall pay the absolute value of that amount to the higher earner.

One of the benefits of having an attorney is that they will have the program so that obtaining the calculation does not involve you personally using the formula above.

Another common question is how long will child support last? In San Diego, the Judges order child support in the following manner: 18 years of age plus graduation from high school, or 19 if in high school full-time, or past 18 or 19 years of age for special needs children.

CHAPTER ELEVEN
HOW IS THE AMOUNT OF SPOUSAL SUPPORT DETERMINED AND HOW LONG WILL IT LAST?

Another common question is how much spousal support will I have to pay or how much spousal support will I receive? For temporary spousal support orders [pre-judgment], my experience is that the Judges in San Diego use the same program {Disso Master} for the calculation. For permanent support orders, the Judges use the following factors: Two Family Law Codes: 4320 and 4336. These codes are not listed in their entirety. However, important factors have been "lifted" from the Code for your educational purposes. This is a very complicated area of the law and the Judges have wide discretion in both temporary and permanent spousal support orders. Below is a specific list of the factors which the San Diego Judges consider in permanent spousal support so that your strategies and techniques [whether payor or payee] will be consistent with your goals.

In ordering spousal support, the court shall consider the following circumstances: the extent to which the earning capacity of each party is sufficient to maintain the standard of living established during the marriage, taking into account all of the following: the marketable skills of the supported party; the job market for those skills; the time and expenses required for the supported party to acquire the appropriate education or training to develop those skills; and the possible need for retraining or education to acquire other, more marketable skills or employment. In addition, the Court takes into account the following as to the extent to which the supported party's present or future earning capacity is impaired by periods of unemployment that were incurred during the marriage to permit the supported party to devote time to domestic duties; the extent to which the supported party contributed to the attainment of an education, training, career position, or a license by the supporting party and the ability of the supporting party to pay spousal support, taking into account the supporting party's earning capacity, earned and unearned income, assets, and standard of living. Furthermore, the Court takes into account the needs of each party based on the standard of living established during the marriage as well as the obligations and assets, including the separate property of each party.

The duration of the marriage is a very important consideration since a marriage of more than ten [10] years is considered a "long term marriage" and the presumption is that there is indefinite jurisdiction to award spousal support and not one-half of the length of the marriage. This rule applies to cases in divorce or legal separation proceedings filed on or after January 1, 1988, so this is 99.9%+ of the cases now in Court.

In addition, the Court takes into account the ability of the supported party to engage in gainful employment without unduly interfering with the interests of dependent children in the custody of the party as well as the age and health of the parties.

Documented evidence of any history of domestic violence, as defined in Section 6211, between the parties, including, but not limited to, consideration of emotional distress resulting from domestic violence perpetrated against the supported party by the supporting party, and consideration of any history of violence against the supporting party by the supported party is an extremely important consideration the Judges take into account. A documented history of domestic violence would allow the Judge to set a spousal support award at $0. When no such history exists, it may result in a spousal support award. The operative words, of course, are "documented evidence", and this is one reason of many why it is so important to have evidence submitted. The Judge does not know what is inside your mind or what the truth is and rules on evidence submitted in accordance with the law. As such, this submission of evidence is a crucial component of any family law case.

The Judge also will take into account the immediate and specific tax consequences for each party and will balance the hardships to each party.

As to the time period, or duration of the order, the Judges also consider the goal that the supported party shall be self-supporting within a reasonable period of time; and except in the case of a marriage of long duration as described in Section 4336, a "reasonable period of time" shall generally be one-half the length of the marriage.

Ultimately, for spousal support, the Judge has wide discretion both for duration and amount as one of the final provisions is that nothing in this section is intended to limit the court's discretion to order support for a greater or lesser length of time based on any of the other factors listed in this section, Section 4336, or the circumstances of the parties or any other factors the court determines are just and equitable.

CHAPTER TWELVE
WHAT SHOULD I DO IF I LOSE MY JOB OR MY INCOME IS SUBSTANTIALLY REDUCED?

Recently, in San Diego, many residents have lost their jobs or have had their incomes substantially reduced. If there is a child and/or spousal support order in effect, it is imperative to immediately file a motion to modify the existing orders since support modifications are not allowed prior to the filing of the order to show cause to modify retroactively. Since, given the court schedule of the court houses, it may take more than 30 days to get a hearing, it is essential to file the motion to give the Judge the authority to make orders retroactive to the filing date since the order in place must be followed until a Judge modifies this order. Oral agreements are not binding, so filing immediately is essential to protect the rights of the payor and to try and obtain her/his goals. Many times, the employers will give notice of impending layoffs or termination with either termination packages or other benefits. Many times, as well, they will not. Termination benefits can be considered for support as well as unemployment benefits and any other source of income. Sources of income include, but are not limited to, commissions, salary, royalties, wages, bonuses, rents, dividends, pensions, interest, trust income, annuities, worker's compensation benefits, unemployment insurance benefits, disability insurance benefits, social security benefits, California lottery winnings (and presumably any other State's lottery winnings) and gambling profits. The Court can also take into account the business structure and any employment or self employment benefits which have a corresponding reduction in living expenses. Some factors which are not included are inheritances and gifts and some personal injury awards, among others. In these cases, however, if they were acquired during the marriage and transmuted and/or commingled this may become an issue for division of the community property interest rather than income for support purposes. This needs to be analyzed on a case-by-case basis. The legal procedure for filing a motion [order to show cause for modification of support] is complex. Several judicial council forms must be completed including an income and expense declaration with the required documentation attached. If the declarant is employed, then the form requires copies of the last three pay stubs. If the declarant is self employed, then there is a requirement of a profit and loss form and/or tax returns. For some declarants, there may need to be a production of both if they are a corporation and are basically using this as an "alter ego" for doing business. Once the judicial council forms are properly completed, then they need to be filed with a fee of $40 payable to the Clerk of the Court. If the filing party is indigent, then they can apply for a waiver of the fees. In addition, a proof of personal service will need to be filed if this is a post-judgment motion in San Diego County as this is the local procedure for service. These can become very complicated hearings since [often] the payee believes that the payor is intentionally diminishing or reducing their income to pay less support. Many times, there are allegations of cash payments which are not recorded and work which is not reported. Payees can ask for a vocational evaluation if they would like an earning ability to be used, instead of actual earnings if they believe a payor is working below her/his earning ability or they can produce evidence that the payor could make money by citing information from such as employment agencies, newspaper ads and others. Child support, in the family law courts in San Diegoincluding Vista, Chula Vista and El Cajon, is calculated using the Disso Master program which is the State of

California guideline and calculates child support. Any payor or payee should analyze the guideline support before filing any motions since there have been cases of payors filing [believing their payment will decrease] and their support payment is increased and payee's filing [believing their payment will increase] and their support payment is decreased.

CHAPTER THIRTEEN
HOW ARE OUR ASSETS AND DEBTS DIVIDED?

In San Diego, the laws of the State of California apply. All States have different laws and each attorney has to be licensed in each state they practice. In California, we have three classifications and they are as follows: community property, quasi-community property, and separate property. Community property is defined as property acquired from the date of marriage to the date of separation. Quasi-community property is property which would be considered community property in California however is located outside the State of California. Separate property is defined as property which was acquired before the date of marriage or after the date of separation. Community property is divided, with some limited exceptions, one-half each. California is a no fault state so infidelity is not an issue. The analysis, however, does not end with the classification or characterization of the property, as some property acquired from date of marriage to date of separation is not divided one-half each such as inheritances or gifts. In addition, there may be reimbursement issues to be considered. This is a complicated area and it is crucial to analyze the schedule of assets and debts. This is mandatory for the preliminary declaration of disclosure for all family law cases in San Diego to insure that all assets are listed and that the correct valuations are made. The law will divide each asset in one half. However, many spouses do not want to do this and instead equalize any differences. As such, it is also extremely important not to equalize tax paid accounts and tax deferred accounts with each other. Debts are also divided, with some limited exceptions, one half each. One issue which arises in many cases is when a house is not divided in one-half [sold] and one party "buys out" the other. In this instance, it is important to make sure that this transaction is with a licensed and bonded escrow company and that the interspousal transfer deed and the refinance happen simultaneously, as no spouse wants to owe money on a residence which they do not own. There are cases in which a forensic accountant is needed for the valuation and division to insure that the settlement is in accordance with the law and true values. For vehicles, if not sold, many Judges use the median of the Kelly Blue Book and then equalize, depending on the debt and fair market value.

CHAPTER FOURTEEN
HOW IS A BUSINESS VALUED?

In San Diego, many divorce and legal separation cases involve the valuation of a business interest. Unlike many assets in a divorce, a business may not be able to be divided "in kind" for distribution purposes. If there is no division "in kind", then there needs to be a fair market value assigned for distribution purposes. In the Trial Courts in San Diego, El Cajon, Vista and Chula Vista, the Judges often require an expert opinion as to the valuation of a business. This can be one of the most crucial elements of any divorce or legal separation case. The definition of "fair market value" by the United States Treasury Regulations is one which is used in California on a regular basis. This is a price at which the business would be transferred from seller to buyer, with neither party being under any compulsion to buy or sell and both having knowledge which is reasonable of the relevant facts. In divorce and legal separation cases in San Diego, both sides must act in good faith and make full disclosures. There is also the fiduciary duty of spouses to consider not included in the above government definition. There are, in many cases, issues with undisclosed earnings either in cash or in trade for services, or simply cashing checks rather than depositing them into the business account. This is an issue almost always raised by the non-owner and non-operator spouse of the business. This non-disclosure can affect significant decisions by the Judge, including attorney fees, child and spousal support, and the amount of the division for valuation purposes. As such, it is essential to have all of the information. Our firm uses the following strategies to obtain this information: written interrogatories; request for production of documents, request for admissions, subpoenas, and depositions as well as the use of experts in different fields and different disciplines. For self employment cases, sole proprietorships, corporations, partnerships and other business entities, the valuation of the business for community property division can be very complicated and outside the expertise of the divorce attorney. Forensic Certified Public Accountants are used for the complicated job of tracing as well as valuation. Some of the procedures used are: review of personal and corporate tax returns, books and official records of the business, cash receipt journals, deposit slips, financial statements, check registers and cancelled checks. This analysis should also include expenses paid for by the business, such as a mortgage, vehicle, credit card, property taxes, medical insurance, dental insurance, utility payments, food, personal care, vacations, entertainment, IRA and retirement contributions, repairs and other transportation. This is a partial list only for example purposes. One issue is always cash payments which are not deposited in the bank or reported in the financial statements or recorded on any book or ledger. The document collection in these cases can run to thousands of pages. It is essential to have an organization system in place. As many copies may need to be made, one strategy is to scan all of the documents and organize them onto a CD Rom. This is very inexpensive when copies need to be made of thousands of documents and also organizes them by subject and other criteria. A corollary strategy is the use of a "Special Master" for the purpose of valuation as well as tracing and all the other community property asset and debt division issues.

CHAPTER FIFTEEN
HOW DOES THE PAYMENT OF ATTORNEY FEES WORK?

In San Diego, many of the divorce and legal separation cases have the issue of attorney fees. This can be an extremely contentious and bitter issue in many custody, visitation, child support, and spousal support cases and also can be a factor in the division of assets and debts. Attorney fees can be asked for as both a temporary order in an Order to Show Cause as well as at Trial or part of a settlement.

There are many factors and theories regarding attorney fees. Some of the most common are: nature of the litigation, responsibility undertaken, financial circumstances of paying spouse, time consumed in preparing for court hearings and other necessary legal tasks, the necessity for skill in legal training, the difficulty of the case, the success of the attorney's efforts; the reasonableness [or non reasonableness] of the party, who is the prevailing party, and many other factors. This is a very complicated area and needs careful and deliberate attention. One of the underpinnings of the legal system in family law is the ability for each side to be able to afford an attorney to have a "level playing field" in litigation. In some limited areas of the law, an attorney may be appointed for representation such as in a criminal defense case or a juvenile dependency case. However, there is no such provision under the law for divorce and legal separation cases. There is a provision for the appointment of counsel for cases in which paternity is being disputed. As such, it is important for both parties to have legal representation and not to be forced into self-representation or in "pro per" as this is sometimes referred to. One of the most significant factors is the disparity [difference] in incomes. As above, the financial circumstances are one of the most significant factors. This needs to be analyzed in a support case, as to what is the actual disparity pre-support payment and also post-support payment. As the Disso Master guideline for child support calculations and temporary spousal support calculations will be used by the Judge in setting the actual amount, many Judges now consider disparity in post-support payment and not pre-support payment. This is a complicated analysis, and the attorney and client need to review the Disso Master printout to determine the post support payment disparity [if any] prior to making an argument for attorney fees. The Court may order any award of attorney fees from either community property, quasi-community property or separate property. This can come from community income, separate income, principal, or interest income from any source.

CHAPTER SIXTEEN
HOW CAN I GET INFORMATION IF I THINK THE OTHER PARTY IS LYING?

In many cases, one spouse believes the other is lying or misrepresenting the existence or value of an asset or debt. The strategy for this is to engage in discovery, which allows information to be obtained. This can be done in many ways. First, as above, each party has to provide the schedule of assets and debts. Second, a request is made for written interrogatories which requires the answers to standard questions. Third, a request is made for special interrogatories, which require the answers to specific questions. Fourth, a request for production of documents is made, which requires documents to be produced. Fifth, a request for admissions is made, which requires the spouse to either admit or deny a specific allegation. Sixth, a deposition, which is testimony under oath but in the attorney's office and not in the court house, is made. Seventh, a subpoena may be sent to third parties to obtain information. Eighth, an asset search may be needed. Ninth, a private investigator can be hired to obtain evidence. There are many other strategies as well, and a careful analysis of the costs must be done prior to instituting any discovery plan.

CHAPTER SEVENTEEN
WHAT QUESTIONS SHOULD I BE ASKING TO MAKE THE MOST INFORMED AND INTELLIGENT DECISIONS REGARDING MY CASE?

This is a very important question often asked in attorney offices in San Diego. It is difficult when you are unfamiliar with a practice or procedure to not know what questions to ask. This is one of the best reasons for a free consultation with an attorney. One of the jobs of the attorney is to "issue spot" which means to analyze each individual case for issues and then inform the client of a realistic expectation. For example, many clients do not know that student loans [even if taken out during the marriage] are still considered separate property in most cases, unless the loan was incurred more than ten years ago. Another example is that many clients do not understand that their new mate's income is not added to their income for support purposes. Listing their new mate's income would result in a lower support order if they are the payor, since their net income would be reduced because their joint income would have a higher tax rate. Every case is different and has to be individually analyzed. All of the facts must be discussed in relation to the family law code to implement an appropriate strategy.

CHAPTER 18
WHAT IS A LEGAL INSIDER?

In my opinion, a legal insider is a person who has knowledge which persons who are not familiar with the law do not have. For San Diego, California, this includes attorneys who practice regularly in the San Diego Court Houses. More specifically, for family law, this includes attorneys who make numerous court appearances every month in the main court house in downtown San Diego, in the Madge Bradley court house in downtown San Diego, in the Vista court house, in the Chula Vista court house and in the El Cajon court house. My current family law practice is limited to San Diego County. My complete resume is listed on my website, which is **www.divorce.help411.com,** and I believe I am a legal insider given my training, education, and experience in the San Diego Court System.

CHAPTER 19
LEGAL DISCLAIMER

This book was prepared in September of 2009 and printed in late 2009 and is only the author's opinion. Laws change and judicial council forms change as do procedures. No reader may rely on any of the information in this book in preparing for his or her legal case. All are instructed to, at a minimum, consult with a licensed and experienced attorney prior to making any decisions regarding strategies and techniques.

CONCLUSION

Not all questions have been answered in this book. This book is not a comprehensive family law treatise but rather a book in a question and answer format. Some of the subject matter discussed is complicated and complex.

I hope you found this book to give you information you did not have when you started reading and that this assists you in making intelligent decisions regarding strategies and techniques to protect your rights and to try and obtain your legal goals.

1976-1977	Who's Who Among American High School Students
1977	Illinois State Scholar
April 27, 1984	Bachelor of Arts: University of Michigan [Ann Arbor]
1986	National Order of the Barristers
November 21, 1986	Who's Who Among American Law Students
1987	National Order of the Barristers
1987	Recognition of Professional Achievement: University of San Diego School of Law: Appellate Moot Court Board
April 10, 1987	Special Recognition of Outstanding Service on the Advocacy Honors Board
April 10, 1987	Dean's Award for Outstanding Service and Contribution to the Law School
May 4, 1987	Certificate of Appreciation: Director of Westlaw Program: Law School
May 10, 1987	Juris Doctor: California Western School of Law

June 15, 1988	Admitted to Practice Law: State of California
July 1, 1988	Admitted to Practice Law: Southern District of California
November 10, 1988	Admitted to Practice Law: State of Illinois
2006	Peer Review Rated for Ethical Standards and Legal Ability: Martindale-Hubbell/LexisNexis
May 18, 2007	Award of Merit: National Center for Missing and Exploited Children: In Recognition and Appreciation for Outstanding Commitment to the Protection of Children and Knowledge of the Hague Convention on the Civil Aspects of International Child Abduction
September 17, 2008	Settlement Conference Judge: Family: El Cajon Superior Court
2009	Quoted: Money Magazine: March: Special Report
2009	Featured: San Diego Magazine: April: Lawyers and Law Firms You Need to Know
2009	Attorney Pages.com: Leading San Diego Divorce Lawyers

May 6, 2009	AVVO: Rating: Excellent
2009	State Bar of California: Section Member: Family Law & Trusts and Estates
2009	Semi Finalist: San Diego Daily Transcript: Top Attorneys 2009 in Family Practice
2009	Moot Court Judge: September 25, 2009: University of San Diego School of Law
2009-2010	Honored Member: Stanford's Who's Who: Black Book
2010	Member: Marquis Who'sWho in America
2010	Pinkerton, Doppelt & Associates, LLP Directory of Distinguised Attorneys Martindale-Hubbell/LexisNexis

ROY M. DOPPELT, ESQUIRE

Made in the USA
Middletown, DE
12 November 2026

36932793R10030